Dec 2002

A
Genie's
Wisdom

• • • • •

A Fable of How a CEO Learned to Be a Marketing Genius

JACK TROUT

JOHN WILEY & SONS, INC.

Published by John Wiley & Sons, Inc., Hoboken, New Jersey.
Published simultaneously in Canada.

For general information on our other products and services please contact our Customer Care Department within the United States at (800) 762-2974, outside the United States at (317) 572-3993, or fax (317) 572-4002.

Wiley also publishes its books in a variety of electronic formats. Some content that appears in print may not be available in electronic books.

Illustrations by Volker Fremuth

Library of Congress Cataloging-in-Publication Data:

Trout, Jack.
  A genie's wisdom : a fable of how a CEO learned to be a marketing genius / Jack Trout.
     p. cm.
    ISBN 0-471-23608-X (CLOTH : alk. paper)
   1. Marketing—Management. 2. Marketing—Decision making.
3. Brand name products. I. Title.
  HF5415.13 .T735   2003
  658.8—dc21

                                2002014454

Printed in the United States of America.

10 9 8 7 6 5 4 3 2 1

This book is dedicated to those who have had it with the academics, consultants, and con-men (women) who want to make marketing far more complex than it has to be.

CONTENTS

· · · · ·

THE STORY
BEHIND THE FABLE
• • • • •

I've been hanging around the marketing world
for more years than I care to admit. Over many
decades, I've been in and out of companies who rep-
resent just about every type of business imaginable—
from computers to caskets and everything in between, and in businesses that can be found on almost every continent on which people do business.

I've also lectured to business audiences around
the world and have noticed that, over and over,
whether they've been trained or not, people ask the
same questions about marketing.

These on-going questions, coupled with the
highly publicized marketing problems that many
companies are having, led me to attempt to answer
what I believe are the most important questions you
should ask about the process of going to market with
goods and services. This is especially important if
you've just become a CEO and have had little or no
marketing training.

If you want long, complex answers to these basic questions, this is not your kind of book. But if you're asking for a short, easy-to-understand book on what is important to know about marketing, this is it. This simple, straightforward book can be revisited over and over when you're working through your marketing problems. It's a management summary of my many years in the business.

You might find some of these answers buried in my other books, but this book is written for those managers who may not know what questions to ask. Judging from the many companies in big trouble in the marketplace, I'd say there are a lot of folks out there looking for help. I think this book provides that help.

JACK TROUT

The
Arrival

Once upon a time, after 23 years of climbing the corporate ladder in the world of finance at United Widgets International, Byram J. (B.J.) Bigdome became the CEO. Suddenly, his phone messages, his e-mails, and even his meetings increased to staggering new levels. Quickly, he moved from being busy to being overwhelmed.

He had to deal with plans, budgets, egos, directors, and Wall Street. Everyone was trying to sell him one thing or another. At every meeting, when a tough question was asked, all eyes turned to him to see what he was going to say. Being at the top appeared to be much more difficult than getting to the top. But what frightened him most was having to deal with the marketing people. He knew that how the company's brands were managed and promoted was going to be critical for his survival. But he also realized that he knew very little about marketing.

Who could he turn to for help? Who could he trust? One thing was clear: If he didn't come up with enough right answers, his stay at the top would not be a lengthy one. The business press was full of stories about CEOs who arrived amidst a blare of trumpets only to be quickly ushered out to a far less joyful tune. They were starting to rival NFL coaches for longevity with one big difference: Coaches get re-hired. While many CEOs rode off into the sunset with a pocket full of money, their reputations were in tatters. They were widely discussed and written about as failures. Most of them did not find new "top" jobs; in fact, "any" job became a problem.

This thought began to wear on B.J. How could he get help? How could he avoid fatal errors?

Then one morning, as the CEO walked into his office, he noticed a shiny, new computer on his desk. He called his assistant into the office and asked, "Where did this come from?" His assistant was just as surprised as he was to see the new computer.

"I don't know. It wasn't here yesterday and I've heard nothing about new computers. I'll make some calls to our computer people."

Alone once again, the CEO couldn't resist walking over to the computer and pushing the power button to turn it on. What happened next was both startling and shocking. On the screen appeared what could only be described as a "genie." He had on a turban and looked like something right out of an old Aladdin movie.

Then, to B.J.'s amazement, the genie started talking to him, "Master, I am the genie who lives in this PC and I have come to answer the 10 most important questions about marketing."

Not knowing what to say, the CEO could only stammer, "I thought genies only came in bottles."

The genie replied, "That was in the old days. We've all gone digital. Since the majority of our requests were always about money, we've moved into the business world where all the big money is made today. It seemed to most of us that the PC was a perfect spot to hang out. It's got a screen and sound so we don't have to do all that smoke stuff getting in and out of the bottle. This also cuts down on pollution. Even genies have to be environmentally correct, you know. Anyhow, here I am since I was assigned to this computer and you just summoned me."

"Are you going to grant my wishes?" the CEO asked hopefully.

"No. As I said, this is all about business, so I'll answer only the questions you have about marketing this thing you call United Widgets International. No meaning of life questions and no wishes. And by the way, before we get started, all this is just between you and me."

B.J. paused, then said, "Wait a minute. How does a genie become a marketing expert? What have you ever marketed? Your experience is in granting wishes. How am I supposed to trust what you tell me?"

The genie also paused, then countered, "Those are very good questions and I'm going to answer them without charging you a single question. You start by reading the 12,831 books on marketing. Many of which, I might add, are of little value. Next, and this is very important, you study what happened to companies over the past 20 years or more. Marketing success or failure must be judged from a long-term point of view. And, having been around for thousands of years, I specialize in the long-term view. Human beings are very short-term oriented and they tend to lose interest as new things come along. They rarely keep track of what really happens."

Being more than a little suspicious, the CEO had to ask, "All right, but what's in it for you? Why all this help? As I recall in those genie stories, it's about helping you get out of the bottle, I mean the computer, so you can be free."

"Don't be silly," replied the genie. "This is all about investing, not freedom. We genies have a mutual fund of companies all around the globe. We help top management solve marketing problems and then we invest in their companies. Do you think Bill Gates and Jack Welch made all that money on their own?"

The CEO asked incredulously, "Did you help them?"

"I did," replied the genie. "And as a result, we've done very well with our investments."

"Why didn't you guys help prevent the dot-com crash?" asked the CEO, still trying to come to terms with an actual genie as a coach.

The genie responded, "We've always focused on hard assets. In the old days it was gold, jewels, and kingdoms. The dot-com crowd had no assets. And besides, the CEOs running those operations were inexperienced kids who wanted to run silly, sopho-moric advertising. How could you give them answers when they didn't know what questions to ask?"

The genie continued, "But enough of my intro-duction, here's the deal. When you've got a market-ing question, turn on the computer and I'll be there to answer it. I'll address 10 subjects and no more. After that, I'm on to another company. So make your questions good ones. No silly questions like how do I improve sales in Atlanta. Make them big-picture questions. Don't waste my time. And don't expect long, complex answers. I'm going to keep things sim-ple and cut to the essence. As your financial people would say, I'll get right to the bottom line."

With that the screen went blank. All the CEO could do was stare at the blank screen in amaze-ment.

The spell was broken as the CEO's assistant re-turned, saying, "I can't find out where the computer came from. Should I have it removed?"

"No," said the CEO, "Leave it here for a while. I may want to use it."

As B.J. continued to stare at the computer, he thought to himself, "Could this be real? Could I have the ultimate marketing consultant in my computer? Is this the help that I need?"

Thus, began the CEO's journey toward becoming pretty good at this stuff called marketing.

What Is the Essence of Marketing?

"After we launch our mega brand, there
will be no stopping our synergy."

W hen B.J. first arrived at the CEO's job, he did what every red-blooded CEO would do, especially if you've spent your life in the world of finance: You cut costs.

But after several rounds of cuts, something told him that growing the business needed more than just cutting costs. So he set up a meeting with his senior marketing manager to discuss how they could do a better job selling their products.

The meeting hadn't gone on for five minutes before many unfamiliar sounding terms began to emerge—mega brands, subbrands, segmentation, synergy, core evaluators, strategic fit, and psychological drives and roles. Marketing began to sound like a complex area that needed its own dictionary.

Soon, B.J.'s eyes began to glaze over and his mind returned to figuring out ways to continue cutting costs. When he couldn't understand any more of what his managers were saying, he closed the meeting and fled back to his office where he went straight to the computer and summoned his genie. He asked his first question: "What is the essence of marketing?"

The Genie's Marketing Wisdom

"Marketing doesn't sound quite as simple as those numbers in which you love to wallow around," purred the genie. "You can say that again," muttered B.J. as he slumped into his chair.

The genie, with a smile on his face, said, "Do you want the American Marketing Association's definition?"

"What is it?" asked the CEO, adding quickly, "And don't count *that* as one of my questions."

"Marketing is the process of planning and executing the conception; pricing; promotion; and distribution of ideas, goods, and services to create, exchange, and satisfy individual and organizational objectives," replied the genie.

B.J. groaned as the genie continued, "But it's really quite simple once you get beyond all the fancy terms generated by all those books written about the subject."

The CEO, a little exasperated said, "Stop being cute. It doesn't become a genie. You're supposed to be profound."

"All right," replied the genie, "Marketing is simply figuring out what you have to do to sell your product or service for a profit."

B.J. looked at the genie and said, "I know that, but there must be more to it. Isn't that a little oversimplified?"

"That's the whole point about marketing," the genie interrupted. "It is about oversimplifying things and getting to the heart of how to sell your product. Let me give you an analogy. Good marketing is like producing a movie. You put a large number of details together to tell a story. Many years ago, a famous movie producer was talking about the endless number of people who came up to him with their movie ideas. He said that he responded to them by giving them his business card and asking them to write the idea on the back of their card. When they complained that it wasn't enough space, he responded that if you can't fit the idea on the card, it wasn't simple enough to make a great movie out of it."

B.J. chimed in, "So marketing is like a movie with the product as the star. Everyone and everything in the movie is part of telling a simple story about why my product is different and it should be bought instead of other products."

"That's the general idea," continued the genie. "If your product solves a problem, you first dramatize the problem and then have your product ride in to save the day. If your product is the next thing, you introduce earlier things as a way to dramatize your product's newness. If your product has a bigger competitor, you explain why your product is a good alternative. What it should not be is just a me-too story."

B.J. smiled and said, "Have you seen any good movies lately?"

"Absolutely," replied the genie. "It was put together by Robert Tillman, the CEO of Lowe's Home Improvement Warehouses. It's one of the best shows in retailing today."

Improving Home Improvement

The genie continued, "Home Depot took over the category with its 'big box' retailing while Lowe's clung to its small town stores. Fearing its future, Tillman went for larger stores with a difference. He went for neater stores and made a conscious decision to target women shoppers instead of professional contractors. None of that macho lumber stuff. Their message to the nonprofessional home-improvement shopper is that of 'improving home improvement.'"

B.J. interrupted, "How's it playing at the box office?"

The genie leaned out of the computer and said, "How do you like these numbers? In the first quarter of 2002, same-store sales at Home Depot rose 5 percent. But Lowe's, which opened 46 stores in the quarter, did even better. Its same-store sales climbed 7.5 percent. Lowe's profits jumped 54 percent to $346 million in the quarter. Home Depot failed to keep pace, as profits rose only 35 percent to $856 million. Over the past year, Lowe's stock price has climbed 31.1 percent, while Home Depot shares have fallen 19.6 percent."

B.J. commented, "That is indeed one successful show."

The Genie on Budgets

Being a financial man, B.J. had to ask, "How do you figure out how to come up with a marketing budget where you would be spending your money more wisely?"

"I knew you would ask me that," replied the genie. "Let's start with how money is usually spent on multiproduct companies like United Widgets. It can usually best be described as a 'bits-and-pieces' system. Every product develops its own budget. My experience shows that the number set is usually based more on sales volume than on anything else.

"In terms of budgeting, the question that I hear more than any other is, 'What percentage of sales do companies usually spend on marketing?' My answer: 'Enough to do the job.'

"The problem with this approach is that some products—the ones with smaller sales—suffer from underspending. On the other side of the coin, es-tablished products often get the lion's share of the budget, whether it's needed or not. And who is going to admit that it's not needed or it's being wasted?"

B.J. commented, "That does sound familiar. So what are the ground rules?"

The genie continued, "Step 1: Prepare marketing plans that present each product in terms of its marketing life cycle. Is it a new market? How established is the competition? What's the point of difference? What's the awareness or perception of your product and that of the competition? These plans should be candid and based on hard reality. No wishful thinking.

"Step 2: Rank product opportunities. This is where the numbers come in as you determine which products offer the most profit potential if the job gets done properly. Can this product or service command a price premium? Is it a new-generation idea that can help you establish leadership? Is it a commodity business with established competition?

"This step does require educated guesswork because you can't predict the future. What you're trying to do is rate each product or service to determine which one has the best chance to pay off the best.

"I'll give you a rating hint: Rate your competition in each battle. The weaker the competition, the better your chance for success. Competing against big well-trained armies isn't much fun.

"Step 3: Assign advertising tasks. Since advertising tends to be the most expensive part of a marketing plan, it's important to make sure you spend your advertising money where it can do the most good. And spend enough of it to do the job of telling your story to your target market.

"For example, advertising is especially useful in creating awareness about new ideas or new products. It can also be very powerful in comparing your product with that of a competitor or dramatizing your difference.

"Advertising isn't very effective when you're trying to persuade or change the mind of a prospect. Advertising isn't very effective if it's just entertaining your prospects and not establishing that 'difference' in their minds.

"Step 4: Stop when you're out of money. This is where a CEO has to be thick-skinned and ruthless. Once you've prioritized your different programs by profit potential and effective tasks, you start at the top and work down. If all you can afford is three major programs, so be it. When you've reached your limit, the next programs in line are out of luck. They'll have to wait for next year when they get evaluated again. While there is sure to be some gnashing of teeth you have to avoid spreading your available money over too many projects—making all of the efforts ineffective. You want maximum returns for maximum effort."

The Importance of Follow-Through

The genie went on, "Once you've figured out where you're going with your money, you must follow the simple piece of wisdom that Robert Hall voiced,

'Acting on a good idea is better than just having a good idea.'"

B.J. was starting to get it as he said, "What you're saying is that once you've figured out what story you need to tell to succeed, you have to put *all your* efforts into that story, and marketing is the orchestration of these efforts."

The genie continued, "Absolutely. Follow-though is the bridge between good planning and good results. And follow-through is marketing's job. It's making sure that all the details are covered and handled well. Men stumble over pebbles, never over mountains."

"Anything else?" asked B.J.

"Yes," said the genie. "Follow-through also means hanging on to customers once you get them. Here's where you can use technology to stay connected with your customers and give them the feeling that you care. If you make a mistake, quickly contact your customers and tell them you're sorry. Then give them something extra for their trouble. Some people call this *one-to-one marketing*. I call it *keeping in touch*. Remember, it costs a lot more to get a customer than it does to hang on to them."

The Importance of Distribution

B.J. had another question. "Everyone in marketing always talks about distribution. How important is this in the marketing process?"

The genie answered, "In the old days, it was no big deal. You would load your stuff on a wagon and take it to the market to sell. Today, it's much more complicated."

"Obviously," said B.J. "But are there any good rules?"

"A few," answered the genie. "The first is the more direct, the more control. In other words, if you have to go through middlemen, you are giving up both money and how your product is handled. Michael Dell, one of my best students, bypassed computer retailers and has become wildly successful while others have struggled.

"Another rule is never compete with your customers. Once you've chosen a distribution system, say through smaller specialty retailers, don't get greedy and start to sell direct with your own stores. They will instantly lose interest in your brand. Good distribution requires loyalty to your channel. If you want department stores to be loyal, don't start selling through their competitors, the mass merchandisers."

B.J. asked, "Anything else?"

The genie smiled and said, "Yes. It's all about 'show me the money.' The more money your distributors can make on your product, the more attention you will receive from them, which means that it's your job to make your product as attractive as possible to their customers, the users. This means your marketing has to do its job well."

A Warning

B.J. was starting to feel more comfortable about marketing as he said, "This isn't so hard. Just take that differentiating idea and build a communications program around it to attract customers. And then, hang on to them. Right?"

The genie stared hard at B.J. and issued a warning, "It's not that easy. Most winning ideas are hard to spot because they almost never look like big winners in advance. If they did, others would already be using them. 'Great ideas,' said Albert Camus, 'come into the world as gently as doves. Perhaps then, if we listen attentively, we shall hear amid the uproar of empires and nations a faint flutter of wings, the gentle stirring of life and hope.'

"Opportunities are hard to spot because they don't look like opportunities. They look simple and obvious—a lighter beer, a safer car, a store that sells only toys, a pizza with better ingredients. Marketing's responsibility is to spot and verbalize the idea and build it into a full-blown marketing strategy to unleash its power."

"How do I spot and learn from successful marketing programs?" asked B.J.

"Now, that's a good question" responded the genie. "You do what I do: Read every issue of *Business Week, Fortune, Forbes,* and the *Wall Street Journal.* When they write stories about companies, they publish an analysis as well as listing their gate receipts. Reading about successes and failures will be much more useful than reading those marketing books."

With that, the screen went blank.

The Next Meeting

B.J. called the marketing manager into his office the next day, asked him to sit down, and then made his request, "What I want from you is no more marketing jargon. I want a simple explanation of what we have to do in each of our product lines to sell more. Present it to me as though I were a customer watching a movie about our product. What's the story line? And then lay out the program we have to put in place to get customers in the door. And don't forget a program to keep them as customers."

The marketing officer asked, "But what about the cost of these programs?"

B.J. smiled and said, "Here's a four-step program to help us figure out what to spend next year. Follow it and we'll be spending our money wisely."

The marketing manager stared at the program in utter amazement.

 **The Genie's Wisdom:** Marketing is like making a movie in which your product is the star. A good movie will sell a lot of tickets.

CHAPTER

3

· · · · ·

What's Branding All About?

"Our brands are rational and passive.
We want them to be emotional and active."

Perhaps because he was embarrassed by B.J.'s sudden knowledge at their last meeting, the chief marketing officer called a meeting about branding. He felt he could impress his new boss and, at the same time, explain how brands are built and maintained. After all, this was his job.

During this meeting, B.J. began to sense that these marketing people were from another country (or maybe another planet!). Their language was flowery and vague. Words like spirit, norms, valor, character, ideology, and belief floated around the conference room and rarely seemed to come down to earth.

When the conversation drifted into "moderately versus strongly discrepant information" and "unique tags that encourage bonding with a brand," B.J. decided he had had enough. He faked an important phone call and fled to his office to ask the genie what all this gobbledygook was about.

The Genie's Brand Wisdom

When asked about the subject of branding, the genie smiled and said, "This is the one subject in marketing that has been turned from a molehill into a mountain. The last time I looked, there were over 2,000 books covering some topic related to brands or branding. What used to be just the logo and the name of a product or company has now become an almost mystic creation that encompasses unique identities and qualities separate from the product names. There are an army of consultants trying to sell you some branding system or another. Forget all that. But let's begin at the beginning. As Walter Landor once said, 'Products are created in the factory, but brands are created in the mind.'"

B.J. interrupted, "That's what I always thought. A brand name is nothing more than a word in the mind. It's a proper noun that is spelled with a capital letter."

The genie continued, "That's part of it. But there are almost two million brand names or trademarks registered with the U.S. government. To be successful, it helps a great deal to have a good name."

The Genie on Brand Names

The genie continued, "Since brands are created in the mind, the single most important marketing decision you can make is what to name the product. The name is the hook that gets hung on those little hangers in the mind on which people store brands. A good name that's easy to remember has a running start. A bad name can be an enormous problem."

B.J. interrupted, "Give me examples of a bad name."

The genie answered, "The biggest mistake people make is to use initials such as USG, NCA, or AMP. I can tell by your blank stare that you didn't have any of these brands in your mind."

B.J. asked, "How big are they?"

The genie replied, "They are Fortune 500 companies but all-initial names are not really names at all. They're a one-way ticket to oblivion. Another problem occurs when companies take a good name and change it to a bad name. The U.K. Postal Service renamed itself Consignia, a name that had no relevance to postal services. Fifteen months later, after endless jokes and ridicule in the media, it was returned to its previous excellent name, the Royal Mail Group. A lot of time, effort, and money went into that mistake—not smart."

B.J. followed up, "What makes a great brand name?"

The genie replied, "The best names are linked directly to a product benefit, such as Die Hard, a long-lasting battery; or Windex, a window cleaning liquid; or Intensive Care, a skin lotion.

"Another tip is to use a name that sounds good such as Caress bath soap or Nutra Sweet sweetener. In many ways, the mind works by ear so you want to avoid strange-sounding coined names like UNUM,

Agilent, or Zylog. What you're after are good-sounding names like Humana or Acura."

B.J. interrupted, "All right, I understand about what makes a good brand name but what is all this stuff about 'branding'?"

The Genie on Branding

The genie answered, "A branding program is all about differentiating your product or company from the others in your category. As Jack Trout said, if you don't have a point of difference, you'd better have a very low price."

B.J. asked, "Isn't that standard operating procedure for most marketers?"

"Were it only so," answered the genie. "A research firm called Copernicus investigated 48 pairs of leading brands in 48 different product and service categories. The objective was to measure whether brands were becoming more similar and commodity-like over time."

"How did it work out?" questioned B.J.

"Well, I won't bore you with all the numbers," replied the genie, "but out of the 48 categories evaluated, 40 are perceived as becoming similar."

"Why is this happening?" asked B.J.

"Three reasons," said the genie. "There's a shift from brand building to promotional programs or deals. There's a shift from information-oriented advertising to entertainment-oriented advertising. In addition, there's a failure to communicate a *distinctive* point of difference. That moves the equation from branding to pricing. Let me tell you, the first people to exploit perceived similarity are the mass merchandisers like Wal-Mart and Home Depot. They will put enormous pressure on you to reduce your prices. They will get away with it if the shopper doesn't perceive a reason to pay a little more for your brand."

B.J. jumped in, "Why do companies have trouble with this?"

The genie continued, "The trick is to figure out how to express that difference. It's easy if you're faster or fancier or safer or newer. But often you have to find other nonproduct attributes like leadership or preference or heritage. Whatever you select, you use it to set up a benefit for your prospect. Many companies just don't understand this. All they promote are meaningless slogans. Michael Porter said it very well, 'Competitive strategy is about being different. It means deliberately choosing a different set of activities to deliver a unique mix of value. The essence of strategy is in the activities—choosing to perform activities differently or to perform different activities than rivals. Otherwise, a strategy is nothing more than a marketing slogan that will not withstand competition.'"

B.J. jumped in, "So branding is about establishing a brand and a differentiating idea in the mind of your prospect."

The genie agreed, "That's about all there is to it."

B.J. proudly announced, "That's pretty simple. Even a financial guy like me can understand that."

The genie interrupted, "Don't be too quick. I haven't told you the hard part about branding."

"What's that?" asked B.J.

"Staying focused," replied the genie.

The Genie on Focus

The genie continued, "Building a brand is often easier than keeping it from being destroyed by internal forces."

B.J. asked, "How does that happen?"

"Basically," the genie replied, "it's because of the pressures that you financial guys put on an organization. To make the numbers you want them to make, people start to do things that begin to unravel a brand."

"Like what?" questioned B.J.

The genie continued, "To ratchet up more business, the organization starts to lose focus on what makes it unique. They do things that erode the core brand. They chase business they shouldn't chase, such as Marlboro trying to sell menthol cigarettes;

or Cadillac trying to sell small Cadillacs; or Porsche trying to sell SUVs. Sometimes, they create a sub-brand, thinking it gives their new effort some legitimacy. Like Holiday Inn Crowne Plaza—the customers thought that the Crowne Plaza version was a little too expensive for a Holiday Inn."

B.J. interrupted, "I can see the problems of trying to go up-market with a down-market brand, but what about the reverse of going down?"

The genie replied, "Waterford Crystal is trying that with Marquis by Waterford. The more successful the cheaper crystal becomes, the more it will erode the expensive Waterford brand. The same goes for Mercedes. The more cheap models they push, the more they will erode the prestige of the bigger, more expensive Mercedes. A brand is a promise. It creates the expectations that the product has to deliver."

B.J. had a question, "Can a brand be marketed in more than one form or model?"

The genie answered, "Sure, as long as the different forms or models don't detract from the essence of the brand or the concept that makes it different from other brands. If Volvos are safe, tanky looking cars, a convertible version makes no sense in the mind of a customer. If Nike is what the world's best athletes wear, a Nike golf ball doesn't make much sense. You certainly can't wear it. What's saved them is, that to many, it's the ball that Tiger Woods uses. A Tiger

Woods golf ball has sold a whole lot better than a Nike golf ball."

B.J. seemed stunned at what he thought was obvious stupidity. He asked, "How does all this happen? I certainly agree with those examples. But why do those kinds of decisions get made?"

The Genie on Greed

"The answer," replied the genie, "is greed. Quite often, new management arrives and, encouraged by Wall Street, they push the brand beyond where it should be pushed. That's exactly what's happening with the Ritz Carlton luxury hotel brand."

B.J., surprised, asked, "What's happening to them?"

The genie explained, "Marriott owns the brand and instead of owning hotels, they manage them on behalf of investors in return for a percentage of revenue and other fees."

B.J.'s financial mind quickly got the point, "You mean that Marriott can make money even if the hotels don't?"

The genie agreed, "Absolutely. So the incentive for Marriott is to open as many hotels as possible, even in some very unritzy places. Slowly, but surely, putting on the Ritz will become a lot less ritzy."

B.J. had another question. "So how do you avoid losing focus and undermining your brand?"

The genie leaned out of the computer and said, "Sacrifice. Giving up something can be good for your business. When you study categories over a long period of time, you can see that adding more can weaken growth, not help it. The more you add, the more you risk undermining your basic differentiating idea. Sacrifice comes in three forms so take some notes."

B.J. grabbed a pencil, "Okay, what are they?"

The genie continued, "*Product sacrifice* or staying focused on one kind of product. Duracell in alkaline batteries, KFC in chicken, Southwest Airlines in short-haul air travel. By the way, Herb Kelleher at Southwest was one of my best students.

"Next is *attribute sacrifice* or staying focused on one kind of product attribute. Volvo on safety, Dell on selling direct, Papa John's Pizza on better ingredients. Your product might offer more than one attribute, but your message should be focused on the one you want to preempt.

"Finally, *target market sacrifice* or staying focused on one target segment in a category enables you to become the preferred product in that segment. DeWalt for professional tools, Pepsi for the younger generation, Corvette for the generation that wants to be young. If you chase another segment, chances are you'll chase away your original customers."

B.J. put down his pencil and said, "I think I've got it. Branding is putting a brand in the consumer's mind along with its point of difference. The trick is to stay focused on what the brand stands for and not get greedy with it."

The genie smiled and said, "I do believe you've got it. Now make sure your people get it, too."

The screen went blank.

The Memo Ensues

The next day, B.J. sent a memo to the head of marketing as well as the product management people in the company entitled, "Branding: What It's All About." In it, he reported on what he called "a conversation with an international marketing guru." He indicated that, henceforth, this memo would become United Widgets' policy on branding. Any proposed divergence from these guidelines should be brought to his attention. Needless to say, many people wondered for days who that guru was.

They never found out.

 **The Genie's Wisdom:** Branding is all about differentiating your product or company in the mind of your customer.

4

· · · · ·

What Should Be My Product Strategy?

"We're going to extend the equity of our brand
into every nook and cranny in the market."

BJ. found himself under constant pressure to approve new product ideas. Every presentation promised a product that would be a runaway success. Some were new ideas, others were variations of existing products, and some were responses to products being introduced by competitors. He found it all very confusing because he lacked some kind of model or framework against which he could measure these ideas.

He had read somewhere that 9 out of 10 new products fail. This fact haunted him as he was asked to approve products that the law of averages told him would fail.

This called for a visit to the genie about product strategy. How should you develop a product strategy?

The Genie's Product Wisdom

"Now that's a good question," responded the genie. "I don't get asked that very much because people tend to think they can do anything they want to do if they have enough money to do it."

"Why is that?" asked B.J.

"I call it the tinkering factor," continued the genie. "In all my years advising businesspeople, I've never seen a marketing person come into a new assignment, look around, and say, 'Things look pretty good. Let's not touch a thing.'

"When a company has offices full of marketing people, you've got to expect endless tinkering with a brand. It's how they keep from getting bored. The next thing you know you have disastrous new products like blue Prell shampoo, or Crystal Clear Pepsi, or a McPizza from McDonald's. Unfortunately, what people inside the company may perceive as 'improvements' only cause confusion inside the mind of the prospect.

"Let me give you a good way to evaluate products in one easy-to-remember phrase: *A one or two or something new.*"

The Genie on No. 1

The genie continued, "What you want is a number one or number two brand or a new subcategory brand. Let me explain. The basic issue in marketing is creating a category you can be first in. It's the law of leadership: It's better to be first than it is to be better. It's much easier to get into the mind first than to try to convince someone you have a better product than the one that did get there first. The leading brand in any category is almost always the first brand into the prospect's mind: Hertz in rental cars, IBM in computers, Coca-Cola in soft drinks, Starbucks in specialty coffee.

"One reason the first brand tends to maintain its leadership is because the name often becomes generic such as Scotch Tape, Band-Aid, Gore-Tex, Crazy Glue, Kleenex, and Q-Tips.

"Another reason is that strong leaders attack themselves with better ideas or next generation products. Gillette is brilliant at this in the blade business. Every two or three years, they come out with a replacement: Trac II, Atra, Sensor, and now Mach 3. This is why competitors never get a bead on them. It's also why they have 65 percent of the business.

"So if someone comes to you with an idea that has a chance to be a leader in a new category, go for it."

B.J. interrupted, "What if someone is already out there in first place?"

The Genie on No. 2

"There is always a big opportunity for a product to become an alternative to No. 1," answered the genie. "But beware, you can't become a successful alternative by offering the same thing as No. 1. You have to attack the leader with an improvement or a focus on a different segment or group of customers in the category. Coke is for older people. Pepsi focuses on younger people. If you maintain a strong alternative strategy, you an be very successful as a No. 2 product."

B.J. interrupted, "What about a No. 3 or No. 4 product in a category?"

The genie, sounding a little impatient, said, "I said a one or two. If you're No. 3, your future is threatened. If you're No. 4, it could be fatal. If you doubt the power of a one or a two, just look at the success that Jack Welch had at General Electric with that concept."

"How did you help Jack Welch?" asked B.J.

The genie answered, "He was a chemical engineer who didn't know anything about marketing. I explained the Law of Duality to him one day."

"What's the Law of Duality?" asked B.J.

"In the long run, every market becomes a two-horse race," answered the genie. "In batteries, it's Eveready and Duracell. In photographic film, it's Kodak and Fuji. In mouthwash, it's Listerine and Scope. In hamburgers, it's McDonald's and Burger King. In sneakers, it's Nike and Reebok. In toothpaste, it's Colgate and Crest.

"When you take the long view of marketing, you find the battle usually winds up as an epic struggle between two major players—usually the old reliable brand and the upstart. Jack listened and demanded that his people have a one or a two brand in their categories. If not, he would sell them."

B.J chimed in, "So the first step is making sure that my people are thinking one or two in their product plans. What if the top spots are taken?"

The Genie on Something New

"Here's where things get interesting," said the genie. "Starting a new category is a big deal. But once a new category has been established, you have opportunities to start a subcategory. The marketing experts call this 'Segmenting the market.' Charles Schwab did that by becoming a discount broker in the brokerage category. Dell did it in the crowded personal computer category by being the first to sell computers direct via telephone or now via the Internet. Southwest Airlines did it by becoming the first national short-haul airline. This is counter to classic marketing thinking, which is brand oriented. How do I get people to prefer my brand? Forget the brand. Think categories. Prospects are on the defensive when it comes to brands. Everyone talks about why his or her brand is better. But prospects have an open mind when it comes to categories. Everyone is interested in what's new. Few people are interested in what's better."

The Genie on Line-Extension

B.J. interrupted, "But a lot of the new ideas with which I'm presented are variations on existing products. Does that fit your definition of 'new'?"

The genie leaned out of the computer and sternly said, "They're what you call line-extensions and are to be avoided like the plague."

"What's wrong with a line-extension?" asked B.J. "Everyone seems to do it."

The genie replied, "That, I know. But the companies we work with are taught not to fall into that trap. The difference in views on this subject is essentially one of perspective. Companies look at their brands from an economic point of view. To gain cost efficiencies and trade acceptance, they are quite willing to turn a highly focused brand, one that stands for a certain type of product or idea, into an unfocused brand that represents two or three or more types of products or ideas.

"We genies look at the issue of line-extension from the point of view of the mind. The more variations you attach to the brand, the more the mind loses focus. Gradually, a brand like Chevrolet comes to mean nothing at all."

B.J. continued to push the point, "Aren't there any examples of it working?"

The genie answered, "If you're talking the same product concept but in different forms like a BMW in the 7 series, the 5 series, and the 3 series . . . or an SUV. Sure. They are all driving machines. But if you look at line-extension from a long-term point of view, nothing good happens. Consider a study I came across that compared the survival rates (after six years) of 84 new, nondurable consumer products. It found no significant difference between the survival rates of the brand extensions and the new-brand launches.

"This evidence suggests that brand extension gives little advantage to a new-product release."

B.J. Sums Up

"So," said B.J., "In terms of developing new products, I should look at establishing leader brands or, with my No. 1 brand, making sure my people are willing to attack themselves with new and improved products."

The genie agreed, "Absolutely."

B.J. continued, "Next, I should make sure that if it is not a leader, my No. 2 product is focused on attacking the leader and becoming a strong alternative."

The genie replied, "Correct."

"Finally, new products in established categories should look to become leaders in subcategories focusing on different segments in the market. I should avoid me-too products and line-extensions at all costs."

Once again the genie agreed, "That's right. Do all that and your new product success will soar like an eagle."

The screen went blank.

B.J. Tears Up the Plans

In the ensuing days, B.J. reviewed all his divisions' product plans. In one meeting, he demanded that they have a next generation product in the works to protect their leadership. His point: "Let's not wait for a competitor to do it."

In another meeting, he observed that he didn't see enough of an attacking-the-leader product strategy. He advised, "We're supposed to be the alternative. So why are we?"

And in almost all the meetings, he turned down all the line-extension ideas being promoted. When he announced that he wanted more segmentation or subcategory thinking and less me-too thinking, the troops were impressed.

As the managers were leaving his last meeting, one was overheard to say, "Who was that masked man?"

 **The Genie's Wisdom:** Winning products are number one or number two in a category. Or they should start a new subcategory.

CHAPTER

5

· · · · ·

How Do I
Get My
Pricing Right?

"As soon as we work our way through the
charts, we'll come up with a price."

O e thing that B.J. was becoming aware of was that in every marketing or financial meeting he attended, "price" continued to rear its ugly head. It appeared that, at every turn, one or another competitor would throw in a low price to try and grab United Widgets' business. In every meeting, someone was talking about the need to reduce prices or find other ways to stay competitive.

When he probed to learn how prices were set, he was lectured with terms like marginal cost, average cost or demand, cost, and profit relationships. When the discussion moved into a concept called price time customization and bundling, he fled the meeting to visit with the genie. He needed some simple guidelines to help him understand all this.

The Genie's Price Wisdom

"Price has been a big issue ever since humans started to trade," advised the genie. "In fact, the best definition I've ever seen was written by Pubilius Syrus, a Roman writer in the first century B.C. who wrote 'A thing is worth whatever the buyer will pay for it.'"

B.J. interrupted, "I need a little more help than that."

The genie continued, "That's only the starting point. What's different is that today there is enormous competition and endless choices that never existed back when Pubilius was writing. Today, practical pricing considerations revolve around what your competition will let you do."

B.J. interrupted again, "I understand that. But what I need are some guidelines for myself and my people."

"I'm getting there," said the genie. "Get a pen and paper and I'll give you some guidelines."

The Genie's Guidelines

"First, you've got to stay in the ballpark. When markets are established, ballpark pricing levels are quickly understood by the market. As our Roman friend said, 'What the buyers will pay is established.' If your product's price is out of the ballpark, you run the risk of your customers beginning to question whether they are paying too much. This opens the door for your competitors to take your business.

"Next, people will pay a little more for perceived value. Just as long as you're in the ballpark, your customers will take the pricier box seats if they feel they are getting their money's worth.

"Nothing demonstrates this better than Target discount stores. They are competing with Wal-Mart, the killer brand of all the mass merchandisers. But by using designers to create brands, they are perceived as 'Mass with Class.' You pay a little more but you get some fancier items that still aren't as pricey as those in department or specialty stores. Kmart tried to go directly against Wal-Mart with a low price 'Blue Light Special' strategy. Unfortunately, 'Everyday Low Prices' trumps Blue Light Specials every time. Martha Stewart would have done a lot better working with Target. This sets up another guideline: *'High-quality products should be more expensive.'*

"People expect to pay more for a better product, but the quality should be visible in some way. If I'm paying more for a North Face outdoor jacket, it's helpful if I have the Gore-Tex label hanging on it that says 'guaranteed to keep you dry.' An expensive Rolex watch should look sturdy and substantial. But a lot of watches at a fraction of the Rolex price look sturdy and substantial. This raises the next point.

"*High-priced products should offer prestige.* If I've spent $5,000 for a Rolex, I want my friends and neighbors to know I'm wearing a Rolex. It's how they know I'm successful. The same thing is true for expensive cars. While they will never admit it, the reason people spend $50,000 for a car is to impress their friends and neighbors. What does a high price say about the product? It says that the product is worth a lot. In essence, the high price becomes an inherent benefit of the product itself. Lexus sells many more cars than Infiniti because the brand has far more prestige attached to it. But be careful to offer a reason why your product is worth more. Lexus talks about 'perfection.' Rolex talks about taking 'a year to build each watch.' A person needs to be able to rationalize the money spent when purchasing a prestige brand.

"Also, late entrants generally enter using price as a hook. When there's a strongly established leader, new competitors often use low price as a strategy. What you don't want to do is let them get established. You should find a way to counter their price moves as quickly as possible. This points to the next guideline: *'High prices and high profits attract competitors.'*

"Like bears to honey, your competitors will smell your success and flock to get a piece of it. Smart companies don't milk the market. They keep their prices low to eventually dominate the market and discourage new competitors. One of my best pupils on this approach was Bill Gates, which is why Microsoft practically gives software away in order to maintain its dominance or to squeeze out a competitor. His problem was that he squeezed all his competitors too hard, thus bringing the government into the marketing process. That's never good. Whether you win or lose, you will spend a lot of money for

legal fees. Time and energy spent on legal strategiz-
ing could be better spent on product development
and marketing strategy.

"Another important guideline: *It's hard to win
with a low price.* Positioning yourself with a high
price is one thing. Using 'low price' as your strategy
is another. Few companies find happiness with this
approach for the simple reason that all of their competitors have access to pencils. With them, they can
mark down their prices any time they want—and
there goes your advantage. As Michael Porter says,
'Cutting prices is usually insanity if the competition
can go as low as you can.'

"*Finally, prices can go down.* With capacity growing, currencies tumbling, and competition increasing,
the old rules have changed. Prices can head down, especially in commodity categories. This can call for
new strategies such as adding value in unique ways or
finding unique ways to cut costs."

B.J. stopped his note taking and asked, "What
do you do in a commodity situation where there is
too much capacity in the industry?"

The genie replied, "Let me tell you a story."

Turning around Alcoa

The genie continued, "Alcoa, as you know, had a bad
case of foreign competition. And commodities like
aluminum and steel were deemed impossible to make

in America for a profit. As a result, management was busy diversifying out of aluminum. We genies knew that wouldn't work. Making aluminum was what Alcoa did and what they knew how to do well." With a big smile the genie continued, "But a new CEO arrived in 1988 from, of all places, the U.S. government. He didn't know anything about aluminum or marketing, so we saw an opportunity to help him."

B.J. interrupted, "Are you talking about Paul O'Neil, our current Secretary of the Treasury?"

"That's the man," said the genie. "He's not much as Secretary of the Treasury, but he was a pretty good CEO."

Amazed, B.J. asked, "You mean to say that you coached him?"

"Why are you so surprised?" countered the genie. "He needed help and we saw Alcoa as a big turnaround investment."

"So what did you advise him about his marketing problem?" asked B.J.

"Well, we guided him through a simple process that is at the heart of all marketing problems, especially when price is a big factor."

The Reality Process

The genie went on, "First we had to get him to face reality because that's what marketing is about. It is a big mistake to think it's about trying harder or being clever or setting targets. In Alcoa's case, reality was realizing that they weren't going to talk people into buying more aluminum. So, they had to find a way to deal with that reality."

The genie continued, "Next up, they had to face the competitive factor. And they had a number of big competitors."

"What did that tell O'Neil?" asked B.J.

"That told him that with all those competitors, he couldn't raise prices," answered the genie. "Understanding that basic fact of life led him to figure out what he had to do to sell aluminum and make a profit."

B.J. quickly asked, "What did O'Neil decide had to be done?"

The genie leaned out of the computer and said quietly, "The answer was simple. Alcoa had to lower its costs by increasing worker productivity."

"That's obvious," countered B.J. "Even I would know that."

"Here's the neat part. When O'Neil looked hard at productivity, he realized that safety was a big cost factor, especially in an industry where workers are hanging around molten metal and man-eating machinery."

The genie continued, "His successful move was to make Alcoa the safest place to work in the industry, thus reassuring workers that the company actually cared for them. Once they were convinced, productivity soared. Increased production is the best way to operate in a commodity market."

The Results

B.J. couldn't resist wheeling numbers into the conversation, "Did that actually produce better numbers?"

Smiling, the genie replied, "All right, how does this sound? In 12 years, O'Neil doubled Alcoa's global market share and more than doubled its number of workers. In 1993, Alcoa had a profit of $4.8 million. By 2000, the profit had risen to $1.5 billion. How's that for working his way out of a pricing problem?"

B.J. summed up what he had learned, "So, the key to setting a price is figuring out what a buyer will pay for your point of difference or added value."

"That's right," said the genie, "but remember one thing, people will pay a little more, not a lot more. You have to stay in the ballpark."

The screen went blank.

B.J. Publishes the Guidelines

The next day, B.J. transcribed his notes and published them as an interoffice memo to everyone in the company involved in setting prices.

In ensuing meetings, B.J. heard very little about cutting prices and much more about being different and adding value to the pricing equation. He was very pleased. Deep down, he knew that this would help his bottom line and increase his chances of hanging on to his job.

The Genie's Wisdom: A price is what a customer will pay for your point of difference and what your competitors will let you charge.

Are There Limits to Growth?

"When it comes to your stock, sales going up is good,
more up is better, and always up is best."

B J. had his first conference call with the Wall Street analysts. Before he became CEO, he spent many hours working out the numbers for the prior CEO. But now, he was on the hot seat answering questions about how he was going to grow the various product lines. As we all know, "Growth" is all the Wall Street analysts want to hear about. If the bottom line wasn't going up or if new products weren't entering the marketplace, you could hear the disappointment and disinterest in their voices. If there was a "down" or "less" or "decrease" in the discussion, you could sense that the analysts were ready to jam the exits in their rush to recommend dumping United Widgets' stock.

As B.J. tried to be enthusiastic about each product line's potential, the more he questioned the reality of his predictions and whether everything *had* to keep going up. Were we doing bad things to make this happen? Are there limits? This sounded like a question for the genie.

The Genie's Growth Wisdom

"You better believe there are limits," barked the genie. Milton Friedman said it perfectly: *"We don't have a desperate need to grow. We have a desperate desire to grow."*

"Most bad marketing is driven by that desire, which is in turn driven by Wall Street, which is in turn driven by greed. CEOs pursue growth to ensure their tenures, to increase their reputations, and to increase their take-home pay."

"Give me an example," queried B.J.

"All right," said the genie, "consider Cisco, a Wall Street darling that has lost 88 percent of its value in one year. They had a fancy computer system that enabled Cisco marketing people to track future supply and demand for their equipment. But a key assumption was *growth.* After recording 40 straight quarters of 'up,' they thought 'up' was a given. Their ever-optimistic CEO, John Chambers, predicted 50 percent annual growth while the market for Internet equipment was falling apart. Four months later, Cisco had to write off $2.5 billion in excess inventory. So much for predicting an endless 'up.'"

Leaning out of the computer, the genie looked B.J. in the eye and warned, "If you live by the numbers, you will die by the numbers. Being a financial guy, you might find that hard to believe, but that's the way it works.

"Another problem is trying to be all things to all people. That growth strategy fritters away resources on side battles, resources that ought to be concentrated on the main event. Decisions are a lot simpler when you've got one thing on which to focus."

"Have you ever heard of a CEO that was against 'growth'?" asked B.J.

"Have you ever heard of Quicksilver?" responded the genie.

"No," said B.J.

"That doesn't surprise me since you're not much of a surfer," smiled the genie. "They are the big brand of clothing in board sports and they've stayed hot, or should I say 'cool,' for years. Danny Kwock, one of the cofounders says that they are not interested in slapping their name on everything like some big companies are. His point: Big is the enemy of cool."

Don't Focus on Your Stock

"The problem often is that management is more focused on their stock price than on the marketplace," continued the genie. "Many have stock options programs that breed a culture of irresponsible greed. This often results in short-term thinking that encourages short-term actions that in turn undermine long-term marketing plans.

Just look at some of the Wall Street champs of the 1990s: Tyco's Dennis Kozlowski bought everything in sight. Enron's Kenneth Lay never saw an off-balance-sheet partnership he didn't like. Global Crossing's

Gary Winnick would still be building telecom net-works if he hadn't run out of money. These three hot-shots saw their companies' values decrease almost $200 billion in a matter of months."

B.J. couldn't resist saying, "Wow, that's like watching your stock price fall off a cliff. Who's your anti-Wall Street hero?"

The genie replied, "One of my serious students was Darwin Smith of Kimberly-Clark. He saw that projecting annual forecasts with the Wall Street an-alysts had the effect of focusing people on the short term, so he just stopped doing it. He no longer took calls from analysts wanting annual projections. He was moving the company out of paper mills and into building consumer brands. This required a much longer view."

B.J. interrupted the genie, "Wait a minute, aren't you helping me so that our stock will perform better, thus helping your genie mutual fund to in-crease in value? If I alienate Wall Street, your United Widgets investment will head south."

"We're not short-term buyers," countered the genie, "We're long-term, Warren Buffett type in-vestors encouraging you to do a better job in the marketplace. Managers with stock options as part of their salary are going to be quarter-to-quarter ori-ented. To us it's about selling widgets, not selling stock. We'll only sell out when we think you're doing the wrong thing in the marketplace. I was working with Steve Case at AOL until he bought Time over my objections. I could see no good reason for that merger, so I recommended that the Genie Fund sell out. That rubbish about 'synergy' never made any sense."

B.J. thought for a minute and said, "All right, what are the ground rules for trying to grow a brand? When do you start to exceed what you *should* do? How do you gauge that important threshold?"

Focus on Your Business

"First and foremost," replied the genie, "is that you should not venture too far from your basic business. Tend to your knitting is an old cliché that people often use."

B.J. questioned, "But what if your business runs out of steam. Can't you move on to another business?"

The genie nodded, "Sure, but you have to evolve in a way that stays connected to your original business. That way you bring along your credentials and your expertise."

"But what if you broaden the perception of your business by offering your customers more of what you've known?" asked B.J.

The genie answered, "Sure. If you're in the tool business, you can come up with new kinds of tools. Or, in the case of Xerox, new ways to put marks on paper. But you have to be careful because this kind of thinking leads to the everything-for-everybody trap."

"Give me an example," asked B.J.

"Take the advertising business," replied the genie. "Once upon a time, it was run by advertising giants such as Leo Burnett, David Ogilvy, and Bill Bernbach. Today it's run by people like John Wren, the CEO of the ad giant Omnicom. He isn't even an advertising expert. He's a former accountant from Arthur Andersen, of all companies. His interest is not in advertising but in growth. He is buying every kind of service his clients may need. In the past two years, he bought 73 companies in his effort to keep Omnicom growing."

"Is that bad?" asked B.J.

"When your business is more about great accounting than great products or great advertising, you're headed for trouble," cautioned the genie.

Focus on Perceptions

"How do you determine what new kinds of efforts to pursue?" asked B.J.

The genie replied, "A brand has to live within its perceptions. Allowing Wall Street to force you to grow beyond these perceptions is the road to trouble. Let me point you to two companies in Germany in the same business, and you can better understand what I'm saying. You might call this story *The Tale of Two Automobiles.*

"I've always admired German automobiles," stated the genie, "which is why I decided to see if I could help Mercedes or BMW with their marketing efforts. They both make great cars but only one has great marketing."

B.J. jumped in, "Let me guess; you chose the ultimate driving machine, BMW."

"Absolutely," said the genie. "The Mercedes Chairman Jurgen Schrempp wasn't one to take advice. He convinced himself that he had to become more competitive by combining luxury and mass market brands to share parts and development costs. So he became DaimlerChrysler and one big mess. The engineers in Stuttgart will never respect those engineers in Detroit. Therefore, they will never work together well."

B.J. interrupted, "After all the bad press, I thought he would have welcomed help."

The genie laughed as he said, "His ideas of help were to reorganize management and install his new wife as a key aide."

B.J. interrupted, "But he still has those beautifully engineered cars to sell, doesn't he?" The genie retorted, "Even those cars are suffering as Mercedes finds itself outranked in quality surveys not only by the Japanese but also by Jaguar and at times by Lincoln and Cadillac."

"That's embarrassing," said B.J.

"BMW, on the other hand," continued the genie, "stayed focused on premium vehicles. They believe that going into mass market vehicles will hurt BMW's perception as a luxury brand."

"Are you working with them?" asked B.J.

The genie responded, "I have been working with Joachim Milberg but, recently, I've been helping another chief financial officer who is about to become the next CEO. His name is Helmut Panke. At a recent news conference, he announced that if you are premium, you have to focus on it. When I heard that, we bought more of BMW's stock. This is a man who gets it."

B.J. interrupted, "How are their numbers?"

"I'm glad you asked. While DaimlerChrysler was losing 662 million euros, BMW's net income surged 50 percent to 1.87 billion euros. This company is a brilliant example of focusing on its perceptions."

Being Realistic

"How do I avoid getting into the growth rat race?" asked B.J.

"The simple answer is to be realistic in your planning and promises. Remember, there are always competitors trying to take your business. Robert Bruner said it perfectly when he wrote about rs having to accept the fact that business can be quirky. Opportunities and threats can be surprising. Good managers trust reality, not illusion."

B.J. interrupted, "But you have to set goals to motivate people. We can't just say do as well as you did last year."

The genie looked hard at B.J. and said, "Set realistic goals, which Frank Typer defined brilliantly as those that are 'Beyond your grasp but within your reach.'"

The genie continued, "What you must realize is that the impossible is impossible. And you don't want that *impossible* kind of thinking in your marketing plans. What you do want are ways to sell more within your perceptions. For example, you can add product forms provided it makes sense to your prospect. The BMW covers a range of different forms, but they all are premium 'driving machines.' Porsche is famous as a sports car. Trying to sell a Porsche SUV makes no sense. A Porsche with four doors and a tailgate is silly."

B.J. interrupted, "So you're against what people call a 'Mega brand' that can be attached to a wide variety of products."

The genie replied, "The more things you try to become, the more you lose focus, the more difficult it is to differentiate your product. Mark Twain said it best, 'I cannot give you the formula for success, but I can give you the formula for failure, which is: Try to please everybody.'"

B.J. Sums Up

"All right," said B.J., "let me get this straight. To grow a brand, you have to stay within your expertise. Does it make sense to your consumer? Does it fit within your reputation or image? You also have to be realistic in your plans: Be sure it's what you can do versus what you want to do. And you can't let Wall Street set your agenda."

The genie smiled, "You've got it, but you still have to have the courage of your convictions, especially when you have your next meeting with those Wall Street analysts."

With that, the screen went blank.

B.J. thought about that for a minute and called in his assistant. "Contact our business group heads and set up a meeting. Make sure our head of financial relations attends."

The New Policy

"Ladies and gentlemen," started B.J., "I want to announce a new financial policy for United Widgets. It's called brutal honesty. Henceforth, I want to see nothing but realistic forecasts about your business.

I'm not saying I won't be unhappy about bad numbers, but you need to have a good explanation for them as well as an idea about how you're going to fix the problem. But I want honesty above all. If it can't be fixed, say so."

Someone interrupted, "But what will we say to Wall Street?" B.J. replied, "We're going to be brutally honest with them as well. After all that Enron and Global Crossing crap, I think that Wall Street is going to be looking for the truth, not hot air. And if they don't like it, that's their call. We're going to run our business the way we want to run it. Not the way they want us to run it."

With that, he left the room.

The financial relations executive turned to his associates and said, "Can you believe that a financial guy made that speech?"

 **The Genie's Wisdom:** Successful companies are never obsessed about growth. They are obsessed about succeeding in the marketplace.

What Is
Good Research?

"This technique researches things that people
can't tell you because they don't know them."

B J., with his financial background, loved to wade into budgets and find something to eliminate. As he was reviewing the next year's marketing budget, he came across a very large number next to the entry "Research." Because he wondered why it received such a sizable proportion of the available money, he called a meeting to discuss the budgeted amount with the marketing research people.

The meeting hadn't gone on for 15 minutes before B.J. realized he was on very shaky ground trying to understand some of the techniques on which his marketing people were wanting to spend a great deal of money.

Besides the usual questionnaires that were being sent out and the focus groups, there were now some exotic new techniques that they wanted to try. One entailed what they called an *ethnographic methodology* where people followed a family around with a camera looking for sensory cues. He couldn't believe that anyone would allow this and, if they did, how could their opinions be trusted? It sounded to him like the only people who would allow this infringement on their privacy were exhibitionists in the lunatic fringe.

Then there were discussions about a thing called a *Zaltman Metaphor Elicitation Technique.* This method probed the unconscious to dig out things that people can't tell you because they don't consciously know them. That was enough for B.J. When he heard that he could be spending a lot of money researching things that people don't know, he stood up and declared that the meeting was over. He needed some help from the genie.

The Genie's Research Wisdom

"This stuff you call marketing research surprises even me," announced the genie. "The time, the energy, and the money that people spend rummaging around in people's heads is amazing, especially when you consider that it didn't seem to help many of the companies who are in a lot of trouble today."

"That's a good point," agreed B.J. "What's going on here?"

The genie smiled, "I looked into this esoteric marketing topic recently and discovered several reasons for the large budgets you are being asked to approve. First, to justify the large fees, research people make their reports very large and very complex. As a result, many management people rarely read research reports and, if they do, they read only the ones that support what they want to do. But that's not all," the genie continued. "Advertising agencies develop research systems to try and impress clients. They wave around phrases like *Brand Optimization Maps* or *Brand Footprints*. They ask silly questions about a brand's personality, how it would dress or (if you can imagine) what kind of party it would throw if it were a person. Or they come up with perceptual maps that, even with my powers, I can't figure out."

B.J., a little shaken, asked, "Are you telling me that all research is a waste, and I should take it out of the budget all together?"

"It's not that simple," advised the genie. "First, let's spend a few minutes on the human condition. The biggest problem is trying to get useful information out of people. Mark Twain said it brilliantly: 'I think we never become really and genuinely our entire and honest selves until we are dead and then not until we've been dead years and years. People ought to start dead and then they would be honest so much earlier.'

"In a nutshell, that's the first problem with research," summed up the genie. "People aren't very honest."

Talk One Way—Act Another

Soon the genie was on a roll, "Researchers may promise to reveal attitudes, but attitudes aren't a reliable predictor of behavior. People often talk one way but act another. When you ask people why they made a particular purchase, the responses they give are often not very accurate or useful. This is why what they call focus groups are a waste of time and money."

The genie continued, leaning out of the computer for emphasis, "Maybe they really do know the answer to your questions about why they make purchases, but they're reluctant to tell you the real reason. More often, they really don't know precisely what their own motives are. When it comes to recalling, most people are insecure and tend to remember things differently than they actually occurred. Recognition of a well-established brand often stays high over a long time, even if advertising support is dropped. Twenty years ago, an awareness study was conducted on blenders. Consumers were asked to recall all the brand names they could. General Electric came out number two—even though General Electric hadn't made a blender in 20 years. Some years ago, DuPont commissioned a study in which interviewers stopped 5,000 women on their way into supermarkets and asked them what items and what brands they expected to buy. If you had gone to the bank on those findings alone, you would have been deeply in hock."

"What do you mean?" interrupted B.J.

"When interviewers checked the same women's purchases on their way out of the store, in terms of the product brands they had expected to purchase, only 3 out of 10 bought the specific brand they had said they would buy. Seven out of 10 had bought other brands."

Buying What Others Buy

B.J. looked at the genie and said, "Are you telling me that all purchases are random? There are no researchable patterns for a consumers behavior?"

"I didn't say that," corrected the genie. "But what most marketers overlook is that more times than not, people buy what they think they should have. In some ways, shoppers are like sheep following the flock—the herd instinct takes over. One of the most interesting pieces of work on why people follow the herd was written by Robert Cialdino. He talks of 'the principle of social proof' as a potent weapon of influence. This principle states that we determine what is correct by finding out what other people think is correct.

"The principle applies especially to the way we decide what constitutes correct behavior. We view a behavior as correct in a given situation to the degree that we see others performing it.

"The bottom line is that after observing human beings for thousands of years, I'm convinced that people don't know what they want, so why ask them?"

Get a Snapshot of the Mind

B.J. was getting very frustrated by all this as he said, "So what can you ask them that can be of use?"

"What you really want to get is a quick snapshot of the perceptions that exist in the mind. Not deep thoughts. People don't think deeply about much more than their health, their money, or their sex life," continued the genie.

"What you're after are the perceptual strengths and weaknesses of you and your competitors, as they exist in the minds of the target group of consumers. My favorite mode of research is to line up the basic attributes that surround a category and then ask people to score them on a rating scale of 1 to 10. This is done on a competitor-by-competitor basis. The objective is to see who owns what idea or perception in a category. You could call this differentiation research."

B.J. countered, "I think I am going to need an example or two to understand this."

"Take toothpaste as an example," said the Genie. "There are a number of attributes that surround this product such as cavity prevention, tartar control, taste, whitening, breath protection, natural ingredients, and advanced technology. Crest built their brand on cavity prevention, Aim on taste, UltraBrite on whitening, and Close-Up on breath protection. In recent years, Tom's of Maine has preempted natural ingredients, and Mentadent has become a major

player with its baking soda and peroxide ingredients. Topal claimed to eliminate tobacco stains, and
recently, Colgate climbed back into first place with
Total, which features three attributes: cavity prevention, tartar control, and germ killing."

B.J. nodded as he joined in, "Everyone owns an
attribute, right?"

"That's right for the successful brands," said the
genie. "The trick is to figure out in advance which attribute or difference you would like to preempt in the
consumer's mind. The research should serve as your
road map into your consumer's mind and around
your competitors' perceptions."

B.J. slowly took all that in and attempted to
summarize what the genie had said, "So good research doesn't waste time figuring out what people
want or probing their psyches. It's really simply trying to measure their perceptions about what makes
you different from your competitors."

The genie smiled and said, "That's about it. But
let me give you one other warning that has caused
enormous trouble for many."

"What's that?" asked B.J., preparing to take notes.

Some Thoughts about the Future

"With all my powers," continued the genie, "even I
can't predict the future. And yet a lot of research dollars are spent trying to do just that. History is filled

with bold forecasts that didn't pan out. That's why re-searching new ideas is almost impossible. People can't evaluate something until they see it, try it, and see that others are buying it. That's why I told Chester Carlson, the inventor of xerography, to ignore all that research that concluded that people wouldn't pay five cents a copy. He listened and the rest is history."

Surprised, B.J. asked, "You were involved with Xerox?"

The genie, smiling, said, "Absolutely. That was our fund's first big winner. Luckily, we sold out when a later CEO named McColough decided to get into computers. We didn't need any research to tell us that wouldn't work."

"But if you're in the technology business, don't you have to deal with the future?" asked B.J. "After all, it's forever changing."

"You've got a point," replied the genie, "but you have to be careful. My problem with Bill Gates is that he was always investing in dreams, not reality."

"Like what?" asked B.J.

"Interactive television," answered the genie. "He lost billions on the premise that people want to in-teract with their television sets. I warned him that people don't want to interact with their television. They want their sets to entertain them. Bill wouldn't listen."

B.J. continued, "Are you telling me that I have to plan on a day-by-day basis?"

"Not exactly. Spotting trends is the best you can do about the future. America's health orientation is certainly a trend that products have taken advantage of. Look at all that drug advertising on television. Also, the baby boomers' preoccupation with looking young, not aging, has lead to an explosion in the spa business. Did you know that 95 million people visited spas last year? But trend spotting can be tricky. The most common flaw is extrapolating a trend. According to the red meat predictions of a few years ago, everyone today would be eating broiled fish or mesquite-barbecued chicken. But that is not what happened—red meat consumption has gone up. Basic habits change very slowly, and the press often magnifies small changes out of proportion. Equally as bad as extrapolating a trend is the common practice of assuming that the future will be a replay of the past. When you assume that nothing will change, you are predicting the future just as surely as when you assume that something will change. Remember, the unexpected always happens. And the unexpected can never be researched."

With that, the screen went blank.

The Next Day

The next day, B.J. summoned his marketing research people and announced that he was cutting the research budget in half. When they started to complain that certain advanced projects would suffer, he announced that what he really wanted was some simple perceptual attribute research on each product category using a semantic differential score of 1 to 10. Then, if they wanted to study some important trends, that was fine. But the leading-edge research was a waste of time and money and would no longer be affordable.

As he left the room, he left behind a group of research people who looked stricken—a bit like a group of children that just had their toys taken away from them.

 **The Genie's Wisdom:** Good research is simple, not complex and all about perceptions. It should contain a strong degree of common sense.

CHAPTER

8

· · · · ·

How Do I
Evaluate Advertising?

"We are not selling; we're bonding with customers."

B eing a finance man, B.J. was always a little leery about the money being spent on advertising. He was well aware of the famous quote from some unknown CEO he couldn't name, "I know that half of my advertising is wasted. The problem is that I don't know which half."

Now for the first time, he was faced with having to approve these large budgets and defend them to his Board of Directors. So B.J. felt a little anxiety when his chief marketing officer called to set up a meeting so that B.J. could meet the advertising agency and hear what they were recommending for next year's programs. A date was set.

On the appointed day, a large crowd gathered in B.J.'s conference room. Everyone seemed to have a presentation of some sort. Some had flip charts; others used PowerPoint. As he sat there without a presentation to defend himself, he felt more than a little naked.

As the meeting rolled on, it became a blur of research, objectivity, pretty pictures, and slick presentations using fancy terms that he didn't quite get. The one thing he did understand was the amount of money all this was going to cost, first to produce it and then to run it.

As he sat there, he realized that he had no idea whether or not all this was good or bad. Every time he asked a question, two or three people jumped in to tell him why what they were showing was not only right, it was wonderful.

And his marketing manager was of little help. In fact, he sounded like one of the agency's team. B.J. surmised that he had seen the materials before and had already approved it. So now he was selling it as hard as the agency.

What should he do? He stood up, thanked everyone for coming, and announced that he had to think about it all.

Then, he headed straight for his computer. It clearly was time to consult the genie about evaluating advertising.

The Genie's Advertising Wisdom

No sooner had the genie appeared on the screen when he announced, "Did all those suits confuse you?" Surprised, B.J. asked, "Were you at that meeting?" "Nope," replied the genie, "I didn't have to be; they are all pretty much the same. Lots of charts, pretty pictures, smoke, and not much strategy."

B.J. replied, nodding, "I got that part, but they want me to spend a large amount of money on what can only be called smoke and mirrors. How do I make sense of all that stuff?"

The genie, in a soothing voice, said, "Calm down. Let me give you a short course on how to evaluate advertising.

"First of all, advertising is what you do when you can't go to see somebody personally. You send a television commercial or a print ad to tell your story," the genie went on. "Any ad program has to start with the product difference you are trying to communicate. Why buy my product instead of someone else's? You're not after a meaningless slogan. Your program has to contain that difference and the benefit that comes with it."

B.J. countered, "But they said advertising has to form a bond with the customer. The customers have to like the advertising, which means you can't sell too hard."

The genie leaned out of the screen and emphatically announced, "That's bullshit. Or as we used to say in the old days, CAMEL DUNG."

He continued, "The basic role of an agency is to take that difference and make it interesting by dramatizing it. People are attracted to the media because of its entertainment and information value, not because they are dying to see your latest ad. The agency can use sex or humor or whatever, but the ad must communicate that reason to buy. If you like the way the agency did that, approve it. Or ask for more drama. Liking advertising is only useful if you're selling tickets to watch it."

"Can you give me an example of the kind of advertising you like?" asked B.J.

"I like Pepsi-Cola's advertising for their brand of water called Aquafina. The differentiating idea is guaranteed purity, which is right on the label. The commercial shows nothing but pure water and the brand. The verbal message describes the product as 'pure nothing,' and they have a tagline that says 'we promise nothing.' They've done a brilliant job of dramatizing nothing. Another is the Bank of America commercial on simplified mortgages with less paperwork. They dramatize it by having a lady slipping love notes to her husband who won't come to bed because of all the paperwork involved on a mortgage application. It is very funny—very effective."

B.J., a little startled at how much the genie knew about advertising, asked, "What else do I need to know?"

Be Candid and Newsworthy

"Look," the genie went on, "people know an ad when they see one. And since these ads are usually interrupting what they are watching or reading, they are not too happy about being forced to watch them. No one likes to be sold. So a little candor goes a long way. This kind of honesty is very disarming. People will often give you a positive response if you're candid with them. If your widget is a little ugly, admit it. But

then go on to say it's very reliable. People will buy it."
The genie continued, "That's exactly what I told Bill
Bernbach years ago when he started writing the advertising for the VW Beetle. I advised him to admit
the car was ugly, but also tell people it was reliable.
He and his agency, Doyle Dane Bernbach, got rich on
that advice.

"To me one of the most candid and effective current programs is the one that Boar's Head is running
to advertise its 350 deli products. They candidly compare their high-quality meats to their competitors'
products. Their concept is simple, 'Almost Boar's Head
isn't Boar's Head.' They've convinced people to spend
a lot more per pound to get that quality."

B.J. jumped in, "I get it. The more candid you
are, the more people will think it's less of an ad and
more of a message."

The genie replied, "You got that part of it and
here's another tip: Try to make your message sound
like big news. People are always looking for news.
News is very disarming, and people let down their
'being sold' defenses. Believe me, if you start an ad-
vertisement with an announcer saying, 'Before you
push that button on your remote, I have some important news for you,' you would freeze every viewer in
their chairs."

B.J. went on, "But what about all those dramatic
visuals they were trying to sell me. They kept saying
that they need these to get people's attention."

The genie once again got agitated, "The problem with dramatic visuals is that not only do they get attention, they also distract people from the message. And when people are distracted, they stop listening or reading. No selling takes place. It's called *visual distraction.* Genies can perform magic without tricks. A human magician, to get away with what he is doing, usually has to distract you visually so that you miss what's really happening. But that's the last thing you need in advertising.

"The truth of the matter is that advertising agencies love to do what they call creative and different advertising so they can get awards from other agency people. You pay for that advertising and, unfortunately, you can't put those awards in the bank."

Be Simple; Be Obvious; Be Patient

"I'm beginning to get it. Are there any other guidelines I need to be aware of?" asked B.J.

"Beware of complexity," the genie went on. "You're not going to get much time from people so you must keep your advertising simple. One message is better than two messages. Simple visuals are better than dramatic visuals. And here's a simple trick. Rhyme things if you can. It makes your words much more memorable. Why do you think people remember poetry more than prose? It's the rhyme. Ralph Waldo

Emerson put it perfectly when he said, 'The road to the heart is the ear.'

"Most important, you're in search of the obvious idea. This is apt to be so simple and commonplace that it has no appeal to the imagination. Humans all like clever ideas but the obvious idea is most likely to work well."

B.J. interrupted. "How do you learn to be obvious?"

The genie responded, "You read one of the best books ever written about business ideas. It's called *Obvious Adams* and it was written in 1916 by Robert R. Updegraff."

"Is that all?" asked B.J.

The genie replied, "Be patient. Advertising takes time to register with people. So you have to stay with your message for a long enough time for them to get it. When you're bored with the message, your customers will probably just begin to notice and remember it.

"Marlboro and Absolut Vodka dramatically demonstrate this principle of patience. One has been using cowboys for decades; the other has made the bottle the star in ad after ad. The last time I checked, Absolut had developed over 700 memorable representations of their clear, nondescript glass container. Both brands dominate their market. Patience obviously paid off for them."

B.J. sat back and ticked off what he had learned, "All right, when I evaluate advertising I avoid meaningless slogans and look for my product's difference. I should judge how well the ad dramatizes that difference, how honest the message is, how simply the message is presented, and whether or not there is some interesting news for my customer that translates into a benefit. If the advertising does some or all of that, it's good. If not, it's bad. Then, I should be patient and let the ad work."

The genie smiled and said, "One further bit of advice, when you look at advertising presented by one of the world's great agencies, devised by great creative talent, and supported by your entire marketing department and you don't know what to think about it . . . go home and ask your wife."

The screen went blank.

The Next Meeting

B.J. called another meeting with his chief marketing officer and the advertising agency people. They all came with the same flip charts. But now B.J. felt much more confident. Boldly he announced, "Put down your flip charts. I want to ask some questions."

With that, he reeled off the key points that he had learned from the genie. Needless to say, by the end of the meeting there were a lot of stunned faces.

He stood up and said, "At the next meeting, I want to see advertising that does a better job of meeting the guidelines I've just outlined."

After he walked out of the room, the head agency guy leaned over to the head-marketing guy and said, "Where did he learn all that? I thought he was a finance guy?"

The marketing guy, still shell-shocked, could only say, "Somebody must be coaching him."

 **The Genie's Wisdom:** Good advertising dramatizes a product's point of difference. It supplies a reason to buy.

How Do I Pick the Right Medium?

"This is how your message will look in urinals."

As B.J. was looking at the marketing budget, he noticed that what appeared to be a big number in total was really a lot of different numbers, some big, some small. They all had different labels, such as advertising, direct response, promotions, public relations, point of purchase displays, packaging, product placement, and on and on.

He was struck by the thought that he really didn't know much about these different forms of media—their strengths, their weaknesses, and how they all fit together. Were we wasting money on some and not spending enough on others? Suddenly, he had visions of money being wasted or not being spent as effectively as possible. These are the types of visions that make financial people very uncomfortable.

It was off to talk with the genie again about media. B.J. was beginning to find comfort in his frequent coaching sessions.

The Genie's Wisdom on Media

"The answer to questions about what media forms to use is getting more and more difficult every day," started the genie, "because human beings just won't stop inventing different media forms."

"I think you need to tell me more about what you mean," said B.J.

"Well, in the old days, it was print and signs. Then it was radio, television, and the Internet. But that's only the tip of the iceberg. Now we have things like urinals, garbage cans, park benches, cereal bowls, clothes, hot air balloons, you name it."

B.J. was startled, "How do you figure out what form is the best one, or ones, to use?"

The genie replied, "First you have to understand the strengths and weaknesses of different media. In the world of advertising, a simple measurement is the number of people each medium delivers to your message. Television has big numbers. Radio has sizeable numbers, but you need more of it. Print has lower numbers and is going down. Direct mail can reach many people but can be very expensive if your mailing list is very large. As mailing costs continue to increase, this method becomes less effective. Billboards and signs reach only a local audience. Media people should be able to give you the exact number of people each type of media reaches."

B.J. interrupted, "You left out the Internet. Isn't that a hot new medium?"

"No, it's a cold new medium that used to be hot," replied the genie. "While the Internet is a good place to send a customer for more information, it's not a good place to advertise. That's because you can't interrupt the program to deliver your message. All you can do is clutter up someone's computer screen with a message no one wants to receive."

B.J. asked, "Beyond the numbers, isn't there a better way to evaluate where to spend your message money?"

"Yes, there is," replied the genie, "but you're going to have to ignore some conventional wisdom."

Words versus Pictures

The genie asked, "Which is more powerful, the eye or the ear?"

B.J. thought a minute and said, "The eye."

"That's the answer I always get," announced the genie, "because you share a related preconception, first expressed some 500 years before the birth of Christ. It was based on what a gentleman named Confucius said: 'A picture is worth a thousand words.' Those seven words—not pictures, mind you, but words—have lived for 2,500 years. And the way things have been going lately, it seems like those seven words will never die. What agency president, creative director, or art director hasn't quoted Confucius at least once in his or her career?"

"You knew Confucius?" asked B.J.

"Of course," replied the genie, "That's why I can say that he was misquoted. He actually said, 'A picture is worth a thousand pieces of gold.' Not words, but gold. He was a true prophet as he foresaw the medium of television and movies where pictures would sell for millions of pieces of gold."

"So, what are you saying?" asked B.J., just a little bewildered.

"If you analyze hundreds of successful marketing programs, you see that they all are verbal, not exclusively visual. They are all ideas not pictures."

B.J. was getting frustrated, "I'll buy that. But where are you headed, all media forms have words."

Two Kinds of Words

"I'm getting to it, but you have to be patient," said the genie. "You see, there are two kinds of words: printed and spoken. We often confuse the two, but there are some differences. The ear is faster than the eye. Repeated tests have shown that the mind is able to understand a spoken word in 140 milliseconds. A printed word, on the other hand, is understood in 180 milliseconds. To account for this 40-millisecond delay, psychologists speculate that the brain translates visual information into aural sounds that the mind can comprehend.

"Not only do you hear faster than you see, what you hear stays with you longer than what you see. A visual image, whether picture or words, fades away in one second, unless your mind does something to file away the essence of the idea. Hearing, on the other hand, lasts four or five times as long. That's why it's easy to lose your train of thought when you're reading printed words. Often, you have to backtrack to pick up the sense of the message. Because sound lasts much longer in the mind, the spoken word is easier to follow.

"Listening to a message is much more effective than reading it. Two things are different. First, the mind holds the spoken words in storage much longer, enabling you to follow the train of thought with greater clarity. And second, the tone of the human voice gives the words an emotional impact that the printed words alone cannot impart."

B.J. said, "Are you saying that media with spoken words or sounds is better than media with only printed words?"

"Exactly," said the genie. "Your primary media are ones that have sound, such as television, radio, and trade shows. Your secondary, less effective, media have only printed words, such as magazines, newspapers, and direct mail. So, if possible, go with a medium that has sound. Motel 6 built a very powerful brand using the medium of radio. They didn't need any pictures."

Public Relations and Promotion

B.J. jumped in again, "What about public relations as a tool?"

The genie answered, "It's very important, especially if you use it before you advertise. People react better when they read or hear about you in the news than when they first hear about you in advertising. The basic reason: They want to know what's going on more than they want to be sold on something. Learning about something in the news also brings a high degree of credibility to your product."

"What about promotions?" asked B.J.

"They can be useful to generate some public relations if they are that type of promotion; for example, an elephant parade downtown to launch your new something or other. Special deals of some sort are good to generate trials for your product. They are less useful if they are just a discount. Endlessly promoting products with discount promotions only trains your customers to look for a deal. Promotions are the right way to attract people for the wrong reasons."

Integrated Marketing

"All right," announced B.J., "I'm beginning to understand the differences in media forms, but how do I put all these together?"

"That's called *integrated marketing,* and it's the 'Holy Grail' of marketing people. This is where you take that singular, differentiating message across all the important touch points in a media mix. Once you have that message, you exploit each medium's strength to deliver it. Public relations can launch the idea, give it credibility, and create a buzz; advertising can rapidly build awareness for the idea; the Internet can offer more information on the idea; trade shows can generate excitement among industry insiders or distribution channels for your idea; direct mail can present your idea to a list of your best or biggest customers; and promotions can generate some trials for your new idea."

"That sounds fairly simple," said B.J.

"It is," answered the genie, "*if* you have that differentiating idea in hand. If not, it will all be a mess. That's why integrated marketing has been so elusive."

B.J. took all this in and said, "First make sure we have that differentiating message. Next launch it via public relations, if possible. Then skew our media efforts toward those with sound. Finally, don't overdo the promotion."

The genie smiled and said, "You're a fast learner for a financial guy."

The screen went blank.

The Next Day

B.J. called a meeting with his marketing managers and announced his new guidelines about choosing the media to carry the United Widgets message.

At the end of the session, he said, "Did you all *hear* what I just said?"

They all nodded. He smiled and said, "I do believe you got the message."

After he left, the head of marketing said, "I think someone else has taken over his body."

 **The Genie's Wisdom:** The mind works by ear. Media with sound is more powerful than media without sound.

How Important
Are Logos?

"Don't you just feel the power of those dynamic angels?"

B J. got a call from his senior marketing officer, who had been talking with a big design firm that wanted to come in and re-do the corporate identity. He felt that many of United Widgets' product logos were old-fashioned and could be improved. Even the corporate name—United Widgets International—could do with some updating. He wanted to have B.J. sit in on some preliminary thinking that the design firm was offering.

The meeting wasn't underway for long when B.J. again began to have a hard time understanding what was being presented. Concepts like glyphs, alpha glyphs, and monoseals were bandied about. Colors suddenly were given feelings. Shapes became dynamic or elegant or sensual. Someone with longish hair stood up and said, "The strong, dramatic angles also help to reinforce a very 'Techie' look. The graphical nature of the design has the feel and mood of innovation and high technology."

All B.J. felt was confusion. And when someone threw out a seven-figure price tag for all the work to be done, B.J. felt that he had to get back to his office for some help. He announced, "Let's continue this in the afternoon."

The Genie's Logo Wisdom

The genie began, "Logos have been with us for thousands of years. A Babylonian clay tablet of about 3000 B.C. bears inscriptions for an ointment dealer and a shoemaker. The Roman legions had them. In the middle ages, every two-bit Duke with a handful of knights had one plastered on their shields. There were crests or coats of arms everywhere. But none ever amounted to anything. What lived on were the names of the people involved or the places the big battles were fought. What does that tell you?"

B.J. thought for a minute and said, "It's not about the symbol. It's about the name connected to the symbol."

The genie smiled, "Absolutely correct. The visual symbol or trademark is badly overrated. The brand's power lies in the name, not the visual symbol."

B.J. jumped in. "But what about the famous Nike swoosh I see on all those athletic shoes, shorts, and shirts?"

The genie answered, "It's the Nike name that gives meaning to the Swoosh symbol. But they've spent hundreds of millions of dollars to link the two. So they can put it on clothing and not be quite as pushy with their name. It's really only a stand-in for the name."

B.J. wasn't sold, "Aren't you exaggerating?"

"All right," said the genie, "I'll give you a little quiz. What does the Starbucks logo look like?"

B.J. proudly answered. "It's a green circle that says 'Starbucks Coffee.'"

"Right," responded the genie, "but what's the symbol in the middle of the circle?"

"I have no idea," B.J. responded. "I've never carefully looked at what is in there."

"That's my point. You saw the name but not the siren," the genie said with a big smile.

"What's a siren?" asked B.J.

"It's from Greek mythology," said the genie. "It's a sea nymph that lured mariners to destruction on the rocks surrounding their island. By the way, it never happened. The Greeks were good at cooking up stuff like that.

"Luckily, no one recognizes or even notices that symbol. If they did, it would say, 'Come to Starbucks and end up on the rocks.'"

B.J. commented, "Well, that symbol which few recognize sure didn't slow them down."

The genie countered, "That's because they went beyond just designing a logo. They were the first national brand for specialty coffees. They also created an inviting atmosphere for customers by designing each store as a gathering place. Starbucks represents a lifestyle as much as a product and they did it without much advertising. Why else would 15 million customers a week pay $2.00 or more for a cup of coffee?"

"What's the worst logo you've ever seen?" asked B.J.

"That's easy," said the genie. "Some design organization got hold of Xerox and changed a very powerful logo into one that literally had the 'X' disintegrating. It was one silly visualization of going digital. That was bad enough but it became a real embarrassment when the company itself started to have trouble. They had created a logo that visually reminded people that the company was coming apart."

"That must have been embarrassing," said B.J. "What happened?"

"Well," replied the genie, "the new CEO recognized the problem and restored the old logo."

Some Research on Symbols

B.J. questioned the genie, "Are you saying that millions of dollars spent on those crazy symbols is a waste?"

The genie answered, "For the most part, that's probably true. I once saw a piece of research on names and logos versus just the logos with the names taken away. You would be amazed at just how few logos are recognized without the name. Only a handful. Yet millions have been spent on logos like the General Electric monogram, the CBS eye, or the Mercedes three-pointed star. And these symbols took years to establish. Your brand-new symbol probably has no chance of standing alone without your name."

B.J. interrupted, "But I see many successful logos such as Mobil or Hertz or IBM. What about them?"

The genie explained, "All of those feature the name, not the symbol. Mobil has a red O. Hertz and Federal Express are unique typography. The symbol that comes with American Airlines is simply AA with a set of wings in the middle. You could say in designing a logo, it's actually the name."

The genie was just getting warmed up as he continued, "There are other considerations in designing a logo. One is the shape. It should be rectangular because that is how you can see it best with your two eyes. If it's too vertical or too horizontal it's not as readable. The biggest mistake people make is allowing their logos to be hard to read."

B.J. asked, "How does that happen?"

"Well," answered the genie, "Some people, if you can believe it, use symbols that are bigger than the name. Others let designers pick a typeface to express what they feel are the attributes of the brand rather than its ability to be read quickly. Some chose typefaces that are illegible. Legibility is the most important aspect to look for in selecting a logo."

B.J. jumped in, "You mean that exaggerated type styles or designs must never sacrifice legibility. No matter how cute, if it's tough to read, forget about it."

"Exactly," said the genie.

The Genie on Shape

"What about unique shapes? Can that be part of a brand's identity?" asked B.J.

"Absolutely," said the genie. "Take Absolut Vodka. Their unique bottle shape is really their logo. And they've dramatized it with their visual advertising on the shape."

"Can you give me any other examples of this approach?" queried B.J. who was really getting interested.

"The Jaguar automobile also has a unique shape which functions like a logo that people quickly recognize. Jaguar is now owned by Ford and I'm beginning to see that shape being modified. That could be an enormous mistake.

"The same goes for Volvo's unique tank-like style that supports their concept of safety. If they change that shape, they are driving the wrong way."

The Genie on Color

B.J. had another question, "What about selecting colors? These design guys went on a great deal about color."

The genie replied, "They're right about color. The warm colors, such as red, orange, and yellow, tend to jump out at you and attract attention. They have high energy and are good for retail. Blues are cool and conservative. They recede to the eye and are subdued and corporate. Black and gold are considered upscale. Bright colors are often described as casual and playful."

B.J. continued, "Can you preempt a color so that it becomes part of your identity?"

"Absolutely," said the genie, "Hertz is yellow. Avis is red. Kodak is yellow. Fuji is green. Coke is red. Pepsi is blue. FedEx is red and purple. UPS is brown. Color can be a powerful way to identify your brand. Just make sure you don't pick your competitor's color."

The Genie on Nicknames

B.J. asked, "What about logos that aren't full names? Like initials. Is that the way to go?"

The genie answered, "As I've taught you about brand names, beware of meaningless initials. They only make good logos if they are nicknames of an established company name. General Electric is a long name so GE makes an excellent logo, because it's what people will use as a nickname. The same goes for FedEx instead of Federal Express or IBM instead of International Business Machines. Can you imagine trying to drag around a name like Minnesota Mining and Manufacturing? It's no wonder they became the 3M Company."

B.J. responded, "So, if I have a long name, it might be useful to design a logo around its nickname or initials?"

"That's right," said the genie. "But remember, nicknames are given to you by the marketplace. It should be what people tend to call you. Don't try to force it. If people tend to use your full name, that's your name and that's what should be your logo. Metropolitan Life Insurance can be MetLife. But New York Life will always be New York Life."

B.J. sat there for a minute and then observed, "So in picking a logo, it's all about the name, and making sure it's readable. The color and the typography are far more important than some meaningless symbol unless that symbol represents my nickname and my nickname is only a nickname if it is used."

The genie commented, "That's about all there is to it. See how much money I've just saved you. But that was an easy question that common sense could have answered for you. By the way, in case you've lost track, that was the ninth question. You only have one question left. Think before you ask."

The screen went blank.

B.J. Returns to the Meeting

B.J. called the meeting to order and asked to see once again some of the designs being contemplated and to hear the rationale behind the changes.

When obscure language began, he quickly interrupted with the comment, "Please, use simple words, no jargon." He critiqued some designs as not being readable enough. He turned thumbs down on almost all the meaningless symbols and suggested that, with more available space, the names could be bigger.

This part pleased him the most: He suggested that since things were becoming simpler than before, the cost should be considerably less. With that he left the meeting feeling a lot more comfortable than when the day had begun.

The folks he left behind were considerably less comfortable.

The Genie's Wisdom: The name is far more powerful than a symbol. A logo should be designed around the name.

What Mistakes Are Made Most Often?

"Don't worry, our competitors are weak, flawed, and incompetent."

B J. pondered on what was to be his last question. It needed to be the most information he could get from one question since this was to be his last question.

Then it came to him. Why not get the genie to talk about the mistakes that are most often made by new CEOs like him. He asked this as his tenth and last question.

The Genie's Wisdom on Mistakes

"You're pretty cute," said the genie. "By asking me an open-ended question, you figure you'll get more out of me. All right, we've talked about many of them already, but I'll sum up the *seven deadly sins of marketing.* I'll also give you a warning. I predict that you will commit one of those sins in the coming years. Most CEOs succumb to temptation. As soon as you do it, we genies are going to sell all our stock in United Widgets International."

B.J. commented, "I'll try not to become a sinner, so go ahead. I'll take some notes."

The genie started down the list.

1. Arrogance

"*Arrogance* is the first sin. It works like this. Success often leads to arrogance and arrogance leads to failure.

"Ego is the No. 1 enemy of successful marketing. Objectivity is what's needed. When people become successful, they tend to become less objective. They often substitute their own judgment for what the market wants. Brilliant marketers have the ability to think like a prospect thinks. They put themselves in the shoes of their customers. They don't impose their own view of the world on their situation.

"But a number of studies show that people are less likely to make optimal decisions after prolonged periods of success.

"Consider Digital Equipment Corporation (DEC), the company that brought us the minicomputer. Starting from scratch, DEC became an enormously successful $14 billion company. DEC's founder was Kenneth Olsen. His success made Ken such a believer in his own view of the computer world that he pooh-poohed personal computers, then open systems, and, finally, reduced instruction set computing (RISC). In other words, Ken Olsen ignored three of the biggest developments in the computer category. Today, DEC is gone."

B.J. asked, "What's the next sin?"

2. Greed

"This is a subject we've already discussed," the genie replied, "*Greed* is the next sin. Instead of building a company, management gets focused on building the company's stock price. This is where companies start to extend and undermine what their brand represents. Enron is a classic example of turning an energy company into a trading company based on how high they could keep their stock.

"The vultures are circling around WorldCom and their CEO, Bernie Ebbers. Just compare him with Dave Packard, the founder of Hewlett-Packard. When he died, Mr. Packard lived in the same small house that he built for his wife in 1957. He bequeathed $5.6 billion to charity. Mr. Ebbers owns 460,000 acres of timberland in the United States and a $60-million-dollar ranch on 164,000 acres in British Colombia. He is $366 million in debt and will probably leave most of his money to creditors, not charity."

B.J. asked, "Can one man's excess bring down a company?"

"Not usually," replied the genie, "But greed is like a virus that spreads throughout the management ranks. As everyone notices the millions the top people make, they begin to feel that they should be making the big bucks as well. Very quickly, they start to make decisions that are good for their income but not necessarily good for the net income of a company. When we genies see a Board of Directors overpaying management, we exit the stock as quickly as we can."

B.J. announced, "I'll try not to be greedy, so what's next?"

3. Ignorance

The genie answered, "*Ignorance* is the next sin. Most big companies get into trouble by being ignorant that strategy is a battle for the minds of their customers and prospects. It's not about a better product; it's about a better perception. AT&T and Xerox lost billions of dollars trying to convince the market that they could be a computer company. This is why I taught you that your research should be all about tracking perceptions and that you should live within those perceptions."

"How do you avoid ignorance?" asked B.J.

"You study how people's minds work. And you never stop studying. My best pupil was John Schnatter, the founder of Papa John's Pizza. He got his 10 questions but would have asked 100. He reads every important business book he can find. He's very good and is building a great company. But he never stops thinking he can get better."

"But how much do I have time to learn?" interrupted B.J. "I'm busy with more stuff than just marketing."

"That's a very good question," answered the genie. "The trick is to surround yourself with people on whom you can rely. My best example of this is Novartis' CEO, Daniel Vasella. He's a doctor, so he went out and hired marketing executives from Johnson & Johnson and Warner-Lambert who have helped him transform their staid Swiss culture into an American-style marketing powerhouse."

"How are they doing?" queried B.J.

"Last year," replied the genie, "U.S. sales grew 24 percent, which is faster than any other pharmaceutical company. There's no substitute for talent."

B.J. agreed with the genie, "I think I understand that pretty clearly by now. What's next?"

4. Wishful Thinking

"Wishful thinking is next and it happens when companies use dreams rather than facts in their plans. Most successful companies focus on the brutal facts of reality rather than establishing what they call 'targets.' It's not a question of what you want to do; it's what you can do. Overestimating the market potential is as dangerous as understanding it.

"A hot shot called Roy Ash left Litton to save Addressograph, once a big player in the envelope-address-duplication business. His strategy was to move into the emerging field of office automation. First, he had perceptual problems of taking an old-fashioned name up against the established high-tech names. Then, he had to deal with the likes of IBM, DEC, Xerox, and others. Bankruptcy was the result of a bad case of wishful thinking."

B.J. chimed in, "Even I would have seen that as a hopeless endeavor. What's the fifth sin?"

5. Losing Focus

"*Losing focus* is a very popular sin. It is also closely related to becoming successful. Rather than tending to your knitting, CEOs start to lose interest and fall prey to other activities. No one better illustrates this than Lee Iacocca of Chrysler fame. I worked closely with him at the outset of this round of saving Chrysler. He was very focused on the company as he restructured management, instituted and overhauled strict financial controls, improved quality control, and conserved cash via mass layoffs. He even starred in the television commercials with that great line, 'If you can find a better car, buy it.' And he also wrote a best-selling book.

"Suddenly he was in great demand and his ego kicked into gear. He headed the Statue of Liberty renovation. Then he joined a congressional commission on budget reduction, wrote a second book, bought an Italian villa, and started bottling his own wine and olive oil. He even had a joint venture with Maserati that failed. We genies began to wonder: You can take the boy out of Italy, but can you take Italy out of the boy?

"Needless to say, Chrysler drove into big trouble and is now owned by a large German car company."

B.J. commented, "Give me an example of someone who didn't lose focus."

"This will probably surprise you," answered the genie, "but the one person who tops everyone at staying focused on business is Martha Stewart, the CEO of Martha Stewart Living Omnimedia."

"You're kidding," answered a surprised B.J., "I thought she was just the queen of table settings."

"Obviously, you haven't kept track of her empire that includes books, magazines, television shows, radio programs, and branded merchandise, all of which generates well over $300 million a year. This woman works 20 hours a day, seven days a week building a living, breathing, human brand."

"Did you coach her?" asked B.J.

"I actually tried, but she took such offense at my saying that she needed help that she literally threw me out of her office."

"You're kidding."

"Genies never kid. She said some nasty things, picked up my computer and tossed it out of the window. It's never happened before."

"So what did you do?" asked B.J.

"Are you kidding? We bought her stock when she went public and did very well."

"Do you still own it?" said B.J.

"Nope. Our problem was that a lady like Betty Crocker isn't real so she can be flawless and ageless. Martha is real so every negative thing she does gets magnified in the press. Look what happened when she sold that stock on what many figured was inside information. Also, she will get old and die. That's a real problem."

B.J. continued, "Tough lady. Okay, what's next?"

6. Tinkering

"*Tinkering* isn't what I would call a mortal sin, but it can cause some big problems," answered the genie. "As I taught you some questions ago, the road to chaos is paved with improvements. Every red-blooded marketing person wants to start improving things as a way to make their mark. They fool with the product, get into line-extensions, chase other people's business, and generally muck things up.

"McDonald's has a bad case of franchise tinkering that has resulted in a collection of 44 new menu items being rotated through an already overloaded menu board. The result is confusion and complaints about slow moving lines at the cash register. CEO

Jack Greenberg had better get back to basics or he will be toasted. He has had a long string of disappointing profit reports."

The genie replied, "Generally, flat or declining sales really bring out the tinkerers.

"Look at Coke and their flat cola sales. What did they do? They re-design the graphics on the can. As if a consumer would ever say, 'I bought this cola because I like the new look of the can.'"

B.J. again agreed, "Yes, it sure is easy to see other people's mistakes, though I guess it's hard to see your own mistakes very clearly.'"

7. Pride

The genie smiled and said, "You're absolutely right and that's because of the seventh sin which is *Pride*. It's a situation in which you are sure you are right because of your company's position in the marketplace. You tend to underestimate your competitor because you are bigger, richer, and, you feel, know more. You lack humility and are convinced that while others make mistakes, you rarely do.

"The most humble and most successful CEO I ever coached was Herb Kelleher at Southwest Airlines. Over the years, he was very careful not to underestimate his competitors. He stayed true to his short-haul, point-to-point concept. He stayed with one kind of small plane, smaller airports, and always had an appreciation of his competition. He has run the most successful airline for years. He has been our kind of CEO."

B.J. stared at the genie and said, "That's seven sins and the tenth question so I guess you and your computer are on your way to another company. Will you ever be back to check on things?"

The genie shook his head, "Nope, you're on your own. If you follow what I've taught you, you and your company will be a big success. You'll make some mistakes but consider them a learning process. Bishop W. C. Magee put it well, 'The man who makes no mistakes does not usually make anything.' And one more thing. Don't let academics, consultants, and con artists make you think that marketing is more complicated than I've described. They make their money by selling complexity. Keep things simple."

The screen went blank and the computer disappeared in a cloud of smoke.

 **The Genie's Wisdom:** Ego is the No. 1 enemy of successful marketing.

Epilogue

· · · · ·

After the genie had left, B.J. continued to apply what he had been taught. As his people began to follow his lead, the company grew stronger. As United Widgets' different brands out-performed their competitor's brands, the company's earnings grew, as did the price of its stock.

Soon B.J. was being featured in the business press as one of corporate America's up-and-coming CEO stars. He was being touted as the next Jack Welch. Slowly, B.J. began to be impressed with his press clippings. He felt there wasn't a problem he couldn't solve. He figured he was invincible and was now surrounded with people who hung on his every word and told him how good he was. No one ever disagreed, especially the consultants who were now hovering around his very successful company. He was invited to join other boards. He started to give speeches and do business interviews about his philosophies. All this forced B.J. to spend less and less time in strategy meetings and to delegate more decisions to others.

With his high stock price, he began to look around to see what other companies were out there with whom he could merge or, better yet, that he could buy. He felt there were other markets to conquer. That search eventually led to an announced deal on a takeover that would double the size of United Widgets and put it into many new businesses where they could use "synergy to sell more products."

Shortly after the news of the merger hit the press, the Genie Mutual Fund sold all of its United Widgets stock.